T0182645

Once again, dedicated to Joanne.

The Illustrated Book of
JAPANESE
HAIKU

The Illustrated Book of
JAPANESE
HAIKU

A Journey through the Seasons
with Japan's Best-Loved Poets

COMPILED AND TRANSLATED BY
William Scott Wilson
ILLUSTRATIONS BY Manda

TUTTLE Publishing
Tokyo | Rutland, Vermont | Singapore

Published by Tuttle Publishing, an imprint of Periplus Editions (HK) Ltd.

www.tuttlepublishing.com

Copyright ©2024 Periplus Editions (HK) Ltd

All rights reserved. No part of this publication may be reproduced or utilized in any form or by any means, electronic or mechanical, including photocopying, recording, or by any information storage and retrieval system, without prior written permission from the publisher.

ISBN: 978-4-8053-1807-2

Distributed by

North America, Latin America & Europe
Tuttle Publishing
364 Innovation Drive
North Clarendon
VT 05759-9436 U.S.A.
Tel: 1 (802) 773-8930
Fax: 1 (802) 773-6993
info@tuttlepublishing.com
www.tuttlepublishing.com

Japan
Tuttle Publishing
Yaekari Building
3rd Floor, 5-4-12 Osaki
Shinagawa-ku
Tokyo 141 0032
Tel: (81) 3 5437-0171
Fax: (81) 3 5437-0755
sales@tuttle.co.jp
www.tuttle.co.jp

Asia Pacific
Berkeley Books Pte Ltd
3 Kallang Sector #04-01
Singapore 349278
Tel: (65) 6741 2178
Fax: (65) 6741 2179
inquiries@periplus.com.sg
www.tuttlepublishing.com

27 26 25 24   10 9 8 7 6 5 4 3 2 1   2404CM
Printed in China

TUTTLE PUBLISHING® is a registered trademark of Tuttle Publishing, a division of Periplus Editions (HK) Ltd.

To Access Audio Recordings for the Poems:

1. Check to be sure you have an Internet connection.
2. Type the URL below into your web browser.

www.tuttlepublishing.com/illustrated-book-of-haiku

For support, you can email us at info@tuttlepublishing.com.

Contents

What Is Haiku?

看脚下
Look beneath your feet

This Zen Buddhist phrase has several layers of meaning. It is found on signboards at the entrance to Buddhist temples where shoes are removed, and over the door to the bathrooms in tearooms where shoes are exchanged for slippers. But the deeper meaning entreats us to pay attention to the immediate world around us and is sometimes translated into colloquial Japanese as "the present moment." We are to experience this moment unfiltered by value judgments, mental constructs or concepts which only act as buffers between ourselves and the rest of creation. When a Zen priest was asked "Why did Daruma come from the West? (in other words, what is the deep meaning of Zen), he replied, "Look beneath your feet." Thus, the great mystery of life is not to be found in some faraway place or religious tract or idea, but in the ordinary and the homely. This is the heart of the short-form poetry known as haiku.

Haiku looks at the everyday, be it the cries of the autumn cicadas, riding a bicycle for the first time, or hearing one's neighbors in the next room at an inn, as captured by the poet Ozaki Hosai,

Husband and wife,
sneezing
and laughing.

Whatever is felt to be significant in that single moment, will be jotted down by the poet just as it is in (generally) seventeen syllables. Deep "meaning" is not a part of the exercise. Basho's famous poem,

An old pond,
a frog jumps in;
the sound of water.

illustrates the concept. The frog jumped in the pond and made a sound. That was it. Basho was struck by this moment and had nothing to add. To do so would have been diluting the moment with unnecessary baggage.

In this regard, it should be noted that haiku poems have nothing to do with beauty. There indeed may be beautiful haiku, but that is not the aim. As noted above, the aim is significance—attractive or not. And this is unique among Japanese art forms, most of which, whether the costumes of classical drama, flower arrangement, gardening, or even the elegant forms of tea ceremony, display an outright or subtle beauty of their own.

Structure

The first anthology of Japanese poetry, the eighth-century *Man'yoshu*, contained over four thousand verses, the great majority of which were in the form known as *waka* (or *tanka*). A waka poem is composed of thirty-one syllables, divided in lines of 5-7-5-7-7, a structure that would remain the basic form of Japanese poetry through the ages. Subjects of the poems included love, death, parting, the beauty of nature, and almost anything within the vast realm of human emotions.

For the most part, waka were written by aristocrats or high-positioned individuals hoping to have their poems included in the various anthologies that regularly appeared throughout the years. But around the thirteenth or fourteenth century, the elegant pastime of *renga*, or linked verse, began to be practiced in poetic circles. In this activity, two or more poets would create up to a hundred verses, one composing the *hokku*, or beginning verse of 5-7-5, and the next composing the following two lines of 7-7, linked often by the season word or nuance of the hokku. The following verse of 5-7-5 would then be composed by either the first poet or another, again linked in some way to the two preceding lines. And so on and so on. In this way, the hokku, now called the *haiku*, gradually began to be written independently, and is still composed enthusiastically, to this day.

The Poets

The first poets who composed the thirty-one-syllable waka came more often from the aristocracy. But haiku poetry, with its simple structure, lack of emphasis on elegance and "beauty," and reliance on spontaneity rather than labored composition, appealed to people across all strata of society.

Matsuo Basho (1644–1694), the best known of all haiku poets, for example, began life with samurai lineage, although he rose no higher than a page to a warlord's son. On the death of his patron, he gave up his samurai status, and likely went through a series of public jobs until his genius for haiku and renga were widely acknowledged. Thereafter he became a wanderer and teacher of poetry until his death at fifty.

Yosa Buson (1716–1783), another famous haiku poet, was said to be the illegitimate child of a village headman and his servant. He, too, was a wanderer, but later married and settled down, periodically visiting other towns to teach haiku to one coterie or another. Through his teaching and art, Buson was well-established, but never became wealthy.

Other well-known haiku poets include Kobayashi Issa (1763–1827), a farmer's son who became a lay Buddhist priest, and who died in poverty despite his renown as a great poet; Kawahigashi Hekigodo (1873–1937), son of a Confucian scholar, an enthusiast of mountain climbing and base-ball, an international traveler, writer and journalist; and Taneda Santoka (1882–1940), a heavy sake drinker, who spent much of his life wandering as an itinerant Zen Buddhist priest.

There are also a number of distinguished women poets, such as Fukuda Chiyo-ni (1703–1775), who became a nun in middle age and studied under a disciple of Basho; Hashimoto Takako (1899–1963), a frail musician and world traveler; and Sugita Hisajo (1890–1946), outspoken editor of the all-women's haiku magazine *Hanakoromo* in the 1930s.

The Seasons

The Japanese have long been intimate with the seasons. With their live-lihoods based on rice farming, it has always been necessary to be fully acquainted with each change in the year—knowing when to plant the seeds, when to replant the seedlings, when to repair irrigation ditches, or when to harvest. Thus, ears and eyes are constantly attuned to the natural world—not to just the plant life, but to the birds, insects, animals, and even the skies that come and go with each turn of the weeks and days.

It is also worth noting that a traditional Japanese house has at least one large wood and paper (or glass nowadays) sliding door opening to a garden, or at least to a line of potted plants. Except in bad weather, such doors are open to whatever view of the natural world is available.

With this careful observation of nature's rhythms, seasons have traditionally been divided, not only into the main four, but into twenty-four subdivisions, which in turn are broken down to seventy-two mini-seasons. Each subtle change in insect song, in the chattering of birds, in roadside weeds, in the color of the ocean or the clouds in the skies was noted and, eventually, written down—first, in the previously mentioned *Man'yoshu* and the following collections of waka, and finally in haiku, where the season word might be no more than the mention of swimming (summer). The use of these sensitive season words will be noted throughout this book, though for clarity's sake the seasons have been divided into the traditional four, including what the Japanese consider the fifth season—New Year's.

What Is Haiku?

But what is haiku? In a nutshell, haiku is a type of short-form poetry, where poems are traditionally composed of seventeen syllables, divided in lines of 5-7-5, focusing on one perceptive event. A haiku poem also traditionally contains at least one *kigo*, or season word. The haiku poets eschewed fabrication, and desired to answer the Zen Buddhist question "What is right before your eyes?" They were likely all familiar with the adage revered in the tea ceremony, that "Every meeting is a once-in-a-life-time-event," and incorporated its meaning into the significant moments or feelings of their lives by writing these simple verses.

The art of haiku poetry has remained popular since its beginnings around the sixteenth century. It is practiced in clubs and literary circles in Japan, and by poets or everyday people in other countries in their own vernacular. Its draw is easy to understand: a poem of limited length, expressing one significant moment with sincerity of expression. No rhymes, no iambic pentameter. Writing haiku would seem to come very close to the American poet Mary Oliver's *Instructions for Living a Life*, a short poem in which she extols the virtues of paying attention to the simple things, allowing ourselves to be astonished by those things, and then to tell others about what we have seen. This was the Way of the great poets Basho, Buson, Issa, Hekigodo, Santoka and, practically all the poets included in this volume.

—William Scott Wilson

A Note about the Illustrations

The illustrations in this book are inspired by *haiga*, the Japanese pictorial tradition which brings together the ink or colored pigments of painting and that of the calligraphy of a haiku poem in a single composition.

Traditionally, haiga are often painted by the haiku poets themselves, balancing the calligraphy of the characters of the Japanese language with an illustration, to create a harmonious whole, where the words and the image share the same spirit and enrich each other. In this way, the poem becomes doubly present, with both aural and visual appeal. The image is not simply juxtaposed any more than the poem is a caption, a redundant commentary. The overall message given by the combination of poem and picture would lose its veracity in the absence of one or the other.

The image that accompanies a poem can also bring a new light or offer a new atmosphere that has the power to convey additional meaning, sometimes unexpected. The visual motif can reinforce the humor of a poem, or add a touch of the unusual—it can open up a space between or beyond words, a space where emotion plays the leading role, a space that is rich in suggestions, lightness, comedy or derision.

In the illustrations that I have created for this book, I have tried to capture some of the essence of the illustrations that are used in haiga. I have made the style sober and direct, based on the Japanese concept of *seihin* simplicity. I have attempted to convey the spirit of things with economy, using only essential elements. My touch is light, and colors— if used at all—are applied sparingly. The graphic expression is without emphasis and the majority of the background should contain nothing at all, in accordance with the Japanese concept of *yohaku no bi*—the beauty of the blank space. The illustrations are created in a spirit of the "just necessary," with every effort made to achieve accurate, suggestive images with a minimum of lines.

Just as haiga can enhance our appreciation of the work of the haiku poet, I hope that my haiga-inspired illustrations will deepen your pleasure in reading the selection of haiku poems included in this book.

—Manda

Spring

In the Spring, the Mountains Laugh
春は山笑う

Spring offers an overabundance of motifs, the essences of which strike the attention of the haiku poets. There is the spring sky, the emergence of insects, the spring sea,

> The spring sea,
>> rolling back and forth,
>> back and forth, all day long.
>
> — Buson

and the remaining cold,

> As might be expected,
>> the Kiso is still cold;
>> cascades of water from the rain.
>
> — Santoka

Spring is also a time of kite-flying,

> A flying kite
>> right there where one was
>> in yesterday's sky.
>
> — Basho

And rice-planting,

> Looking over
>> the new rice fields;
>> crows in the woods.
>
> — Shiko

But perhaps what most catches the attention of the haiku poets are the flowers and trees of spring. The young green leaves are especially attractive to poets like Santoka, and the flowers are noted as they bloom in sequence throughout the season. The first, which heralds the end of winter and the new emergence of life, is the plum blossom,

> The scent of plum blossoms;
> suddenly the sun comes out
> on this mountain road.

> — Basho

And then there are the cherry blossoms. Lining urban streets as well as old mountain paths, these flowers and the viewing of them is so highly regarded by the Japanese that every year there are television reports of where exactly they are flowering as the warmer spring weather moves north. When in full bloom, people will gather on mats spread under the trees, and celebrate with snacks and sake.

Here might be mentioned the saying, *Hana no shita yori hana no shita* which puns on the homonym *hana*, meaning both "flowers"—in this case, cherry blossoms—and "nose"; translated as "It's better under the cherry blossoms than under the nose," i.e., drinking sake. It can also mean the reverse: it is better to be drinking than being under the cherry blossoms.

Some well-known haiku that deal with the subject of the revered blooms include one rather ecstatic example,

> Cherry blossoms, cherry blossoms
> blooming, cherry blossoms
> falling, cherry blossoms.

> — Santoka

Others are a little more staid,

> The cherry blossoms are dangerous
> by the side of the well;
> drunk on sake.

> — Shushiki

Out viewing on a walk.
　Less than ten people;
cherry blossoms in the rain.

   — Shiki

His mouth agape,
　gazing at the falling cherry blossoms:
the child is a Buddha.

   — Kubutsu

Having taken a hot bath
　and bowed to the Buddha,
cherry blossoms.

   — Issa

The haiku poets also found inspiration in humbler spring subjects, from snails to melting snow. Spring goes from February, with plum blossoms and the songs of bush warblers, to May when birds fly south, bamboo shoots sprout, and thunder can be heard. But every day's subtle changes were closely observed, and recorded in the music of the "stringless harp" of haiku,

First rainbow;
　and the plum blossoms?
Still all white.

   — Shiki

Spring Haiku

First flowers, not yet;
winter voices
of pine and bamboo.

初華やまだ松竹は冬の声
Hatsuhana ya mada matsutake wa fuyu no koe
— Fukuda Chiyo-ni

The waterfall flowing down
in one straight line;
plum blossoms.

ひとすぢは滝のながれや梅の花
Hitosuji wa taki no nagare ya ume no hana
— Seio Touou

For a while, I'm unaware
of the snow;
plum flowers.

しばらく雪の念なし桃の花
Shibaraku yuki no nen nashi momo no hana
— Kinpu

The scent of plum blossoms;
suddenly the sun comes out
on this mountain road.

梅が香にのつと日の出る山路かな

Ume ga ka ni notto hi no deru yamaji kana

— Basho

If you don't come today,
they'll fall tomorrow;
plum blossoms.

けふ来ずばあすは散りなむ梅の花

Kyou kozuba asu wa chirinamu ume no hana

— Ryokan

Branches of cherry blossoms
hiding
a bright and shining moon.

さやかなる月をかくせる花の枝

Sayakanaru tsuki wo kakuseru hana no eda

— Yamazaki Sokan

Its webbed feet to the ground,
it gives forth in song:
the frog.

手をついて歌まうし上ぐる蛙かな

Te wo tsuite uta moshiaguru kawazu kana

— Yamazaki Sokan

Ongoing spring;
a nameless mountain
under a light mist.

春なれや名もなき山の薄霞
Haru nare ya na mo naki yama no usugasumi

— Basho

His parents are out
cherry blossom viewing;
he keeps watching the clock.

たらちねの花見の留守や時計見る
Tarachine no hanami no rusu ya tokei miru

— Shiki

Sunset
checked by the sky;
cherry blossoms.

入相を空におさゆる桜かな
Iriai wo sora ni osayuru sakura kana

— Fukuda Chiyo-ni

Its own cage,
a garden of bamboo,
the bush warbler.

おのづから鶯籠や園の竹
Onozukara uguisukago ya sono no take

— Mitsujo

Long spring days;
    echoes heard in nooks and corners
of the capital.

遅き日やこだま聞ゆる京の隅
Osoki hi ya kodama kikoyuru kyo no sumi

— Buson

Drying clothes
    just thrown about;
grasses of spring.

なげやりに物を干しけり春の草
Nageyari ni mono wo hoshikeri haru no kusa

— Miyamoto Koken

With a single manservant,
    plodding along,
viewing the cherry blossoms.

一僕とぼくぼくありく花見かな
Hitoboku to bokuboku ariku hanami kana

— Koshun

A chilly nap; then
    the spring day
coming to an end.

うたた寝のさむれば春の日くれたり
Utatane no samureba haru no hi kuretari

— Buson

Dawn breaking,
    cherry blossoms opening:
the gate to the Pure Land.

夜の明けて花にひらくや浄土門
Yo no akete hana ni hiraku ya Jodomon

— Yamamoto Saimu

Spring days,
    one after another;
thoughts of long ago.

日くれぐれ春や昔のおもひ哉
Hi kuregure haru ya mukashi no omoi kana

— Buson

Mountain camellias,
    falling plop, plop
under a hazy moon.

ぼたぼたと山茶の落つる朧月
Bota bota to tsubaki no otsuru oborozuki

— Dansui

Clouds of cherry blossoms;
The temple bell . . .
From Ueno? From Asakusa?

花の曇鐘は上野か浅草か
Hana no kumo kane wa Ueno ka Asakusa ka

— Basho

Amidst all the greenery,
magnolia flowers
in full bloom.

青みたるなかにこぶしの花ざかり
Aomitaru naka ni kobushi no hanazakari

— Ryokan

Hearing the evening
temple bell;
cherry blossoms, too?

入相の鐘聞きつけぬ花もがな
Iriai no kane kikitsukenu hana mogana

— Masatomo

Cherries in full bloom;
husband and wife led around
by their child.

花盛り子で歩かるる夫婦かな
Hanazakari ko de arukaruru fuufu kana

— Enomoto Kikaku

Cherry blossoms, cherry blossoms
blooming, cherry blossoms
falling, cherry blossoms.

さくらさくらさくさくらちるさくら
Sakura sakura saku sakura chiru sakura

— Santoka

The woodpecker,
    looking for a withered tree
among the cherry blossoms.

啄木鳥や枯木を探す花の中

Kitsutsuki ya kareki wo sagasu hana no naka

— Naito Joso

Airing them out,
    shaking the curtains;
cherry blossoms.

虫ぼしや幕をふるへば桜花

Mushiboshi ya maku wo furueba sakurabana

— Mako Hokushi

Frogs croaking,
    night after night, how heavy
my bedding.

蛙なく一夜一夜に夜着重し

Kawazu naku hitoyo hitoyo ni yogi omoshi

— Cho'u

Wakened from dreams
by a nightingale;
time for breakfast.

鶯にゆめさまされし朝げかな

Uguisu ni yume samasareshi asage kana

— Ryokan

Onto my bamboo hat,
plop!
A camellia.

笠へぽつとり椿だつた
Kasa e pottori tsubaki datta

— Santoka

The cherry blossoms are dangerous
by the side of the well;
drunk on sake.

井戸端の桜あぶなし酒の酔
Idobata no sakura abunashi sake no ei

— Shushiki

A spring day!
Daruma Daishi's buttocks
hurt, too.

春の日や達磨大師も尻もだえ
Haru no hi ya Daruma Daishi mo shiri modae

— Kishimoto Chowa

A Zen Buddhist priest:
the picture of serenity
this morning of spring.

禅僧の寂然として今朝の春
Zenso no jakuzen toshite kesa no haru

— Shiki

With an expression of not understanding
flower viewing;
the sumo wrestler.

こころえぬ花見の顔や相撲とり

Kokoroenu hanami no kao ya sumoutori

— Matsukura Ranran

Even the stately pine
falls asleep;
spring rain.

たくましき松もねむるや春の雨

Takumashiki matsu mo nemuru ya haru no ame

— Seio Touou

Though its flowers are blooming,
it looks difficult
for the old tree.

花さくもむづかしげなる老木かな

Hana saku mo muzukashige naru oiki kana

— Keio Mokusetsu

The mountain laughs,
the valley answers,
melting snow.

山笑ひ谷こたへたる雪解かな

Yama warai tani kotaetaru yukige kana

— Nakamura Koseki

The spring sea,
   rolling back and forth,
   back and forth, all day long.

春の海ひねもすのたりのたりかな
Haru no umi hinemosu notari notari kana

— Buson

Gazing at far-off mountains;
   cherry blossoms falling,
   falling.

桜ちりちり花の遠山見ゆるかな
Sakura chiri chiri hana no touyama miyuru kana

— Watanabe Taisei

Know what is sufficient.
   Consider the humble homes
   of mud snails.

足る事を知れや田螺の侘住居
Taru koto wo shire ya tanishi no wabizumai

— Inoue Shiro

My destination?
   Sake.
   And peach blossoms.

行先に酒があるなり桃の花
Yukisaki ni sake ga arunari momo no hana

— Moro Nanimaru

Is that mountain
　　so tall, or the skylark
　　so high?

あの山が高いか雲雀高かろか
Ano yama ga takai ka hibari takakaro ka
— Ito Shou

Walking around in the wind;
　　new sake
　　one shot.

風をあるいてきて新酒いつぱい
Kaze wo aruite kite shinshu ippai
— Santoka

Well, me again—
　　sleeping one night
　　beneath the flowers.

同じくば花の下にて一とよ寝む
Onajikuba hana no moto nite hitoyo nemu
— Ryokan

Stepping through cherry blossoms,
　　regretfully cleansing my feet
　　in the evening.

花を踏んで洗足おしき夕かな
Hana wo funde sensoku oshiki yuu kana
— Zaishiki

A spring moon
rising
through withered trees.

春の月枯木の中を上りけり
Haru no tsuki kareki no naka wo agarikeri

— Shiki

Traveling the open sky:
the work
of the skylark.

大空へ行くが雲雀の仕事かな
Oozora e yuku ga hibari no shigoto kana

— Sakurai Shou

Walking through the fields;
are the baby sparrows
chirping at me?

野を歩み子雀吾れに鳴くことか
No wo ayumi kosuzume ware ni naku koto ka

— Tanaka Bisui

As might be expected
the Kiso is still cold;
cascades of water from the rain.

木曾はさすがにまだ寒い雨の水嵩
Kiso wa sasuga ni mada samui ame no mizukasa

— Santoka

Skylarks crying;
I awake with a smile
and talk to you in bed.

雲雀鳴くにやと目覚めたり君と床中語
Hibari naku niya to mezametari kimi to tokonaka katari

— Hekigodo

Everything moving
in a clod of earth?
Frogs.

つちくれに動くものみな蛙哉
Tsuchikure ni ugoku mono mina kawazu kana

— Oshima Ryota

Peeing at ease;
grasses sprouting
everywhere.

のんびり尿する草の芽だらけ
Nonbiri nyo suru kusa no me darake

— Santoka

A morning of spring wind.
The shop selling kites
has opened.

朝東風に凧売る店を開きけり
Asagochi ni tako uru mise wo hirakikeri

— Shoha

A good time
for drinking sake:
poppy flowers!

酒のむによき頃なれやけしの花

Sake nomu ni yoki koro nare ya keshi no hana

— Kurada Kassan

Just at midday, walking
with a light step
through the poppies.

真昼中ほろりほろりとけしの花

Mahirunaka horori horori to keshi no hana

— Ryokan

Having quit as school principal,
the man
ploughing the field.

校長をやめて畑打つ男かな

Kocho wo yamete hata utsu otoko kana

— Uehara Sansen

Deutzia flowers!
The cold now departing;
lodging during rain.

卯の花や寒く暮れゆく雨の宿

U no hana ya samuku kureyuku ame no yado

— Tsukamatsu Roko

A light snow; still,
　　the flowery fragrance
　of the tea ceremony.

淡雪のふるも茶湯の花香かな
Awayuki no furu mo chanoyu no hanaka kana

— Kawakami Fuhaku

Spring has come,
　　but even faster
　came the bugs.

春が来たいちはやく虫がやつて来た
Haru ga kita ichihayaku mushi ga yatte kita

— Santoka

Year by year,
　　fewer cherry blossoms
　in my home town.

年年に桜すくなき故郷かな
Toshidoshi ni sakura sukunaki kokyo kana

— Fujimori Sobaku

Drunk on the cherry blossoms,
　　she hates to go home;
　the courtesan.

花に酔うて帰るさに悪し白拍子
Hana ni youte kaerusa nikushi shirabyoshi

— Buson

Wisteria blooming;
my hut now seems
not so simple.

藤咲いて庵のやうになかりけり
Fuji saite iori no you ni nakarikeri
— Kukuu

Children, children, children;
holding tight
azalea blossoms.

子らや子ら子らが手を取る躑躅かな
Kora ya kora kora ga te wo toru tsutsuji kana
— Ryokan

The scent
is in the nose
rather than the flower.

花よりも鼻にありける匂ひかな
Hana yori mo hana ni arikeru nioi kana
— Moritake

In the rain of departing spring,
my traveling clothes soaked
just as they are.

旅衣春ゆく雨にぬるるまま
Tabigoromo haru yuku ame ni nururu mama
— Sugita Hisajo

Though the Nembutsu
is without season;
blossoms of wisteria.

念仏に季はなけれども藤の花

Nembutsu ni ki wa nakeredomo fuji no hana

— Shiki

A yellow Japanese rose
blooming in the mountain;
just one.

山吹山に咲いてひとえ

Yamabuki yama ni saite hitoe

— Sumiyama Kyuji

The bucket for washing my feet
is leaking, too;
departing spring.

洗足の盥も漏りてゆく春や

Sensoku no tarai mo morite yuku haru ya

— Buson

A night of departing spring;
somewhere a clock
strikes.

行く春の夜のどこかで時計鳴る

Yuku haru no yo no dokoka de tokei naru

— Santoka

Departing spring;
in the countryside sky,
a kite.

行く春や鄙の空なるいかのぼり

Yuku haru ya hina no sora naru ikanobori

— Kaya Shirao

My growing old
is unknown to them:
flowers in full bloom.

わが年の寄るとは知らず花盛り

Waga toshi no yoru to wa shirazu hanazakari

— Chigetsu

How strange that nearly
all people die
in the flowering spring.

人ばかり死ねとはをかし花の春

Hito bakari shine to wa okashi hana no haru

— Gengen-ichi

Summer

夏は山が滴る
In the Summer, the Mountains Drip

In summer, Japan is visited by a variety of rains, each type of which is noted, from the early monsoons which bring the water for rice planting, to midsummer storms that send people running for shelter, to late summer rains that forecast the coming of fall. Although the drama of lightning and thunder is sometimes the subject of haiku, it is often the more humble and ordinarily unobserved details of the summer rain that are closer to the poet's heart,

> An evening shower;
> clinging to the grasses and leaves,
> a flock of sparrows.
>
> — Buson

> In the summer rains
> frogs are swimming
> right at the door.
>
> — Buson

Summer is also a season characterized by oppressive heat and humidity, only tolerated at night by sleeping on a veranda, but then exposing oneself to swarms of mosquitoes. With luck, there might be a cool breeze, but if not,

> No sound from the wind bell;
> the heat
> of the ticking clock!
>
> — Yayu

The heat of summer is often enough to cause a loss of appetite and weight, a condition often noted by women poets as something not to be desired.

Still, summer is a time for many pleasures, from firework displays to swimming and bathing out of doors, to cooling off on the porch with family and friends. Add to this the many local summer festivals, with parades that feature young loincloth-clad men hoisting heavy shrines through the streets, food and plenty of sake.

Of course, plants and flowers are given great attention. The green leaves of trees, new bamboo shoots, wild irises, morning glories, sunflowers, pinks and many other varieties of flower—all are observed and find their way into haiku poems. But it is not just the most striking which is recorded; the often-overlooked also captures the attention of the haiku poets. Santoka would emphasize this in his diary, saying, "Those who do not know the meaning of weeds, do not know the mind of nature. Weeds grasp their own essence and express its truth," and writing, on one of his long begging journeys,

> Going, going,
>   right up to collapse;
>   the roadside weeds.

From the seventeenth century onwards, the roads in Japan had opened up to travel, and much of the population, which had been long confined to village and city life, put on their straw sandals and went on pilgrimages to temples and shrines or just ventured out for short entertaining trips. Thus they were able to observe the abundance of animals that thrived in the mountains, valleys and plains. The haiku poets of this early era were among the greatest travelers, and it is not surprising that much of their poetry is concerned with the wildlife all around them. Foremost among this wildlife are the birds—bush warblers, cuckoos, kingfishers and the ever-present sparrows.

As for insects, the aforementioned mosquitoes, along with fireflies, cicadas and even flies did not escape the poets' attention,

> The flies
>   have taken a liking
>   to my bald head.
>
> — Ozaki Hosai

But perhaps the most ubiquitous of the summer creatures were the thousands of frogs (with their singing) inhabiting the rice fields that dotted the Japanese countryside. Along with Basho's famous frog jumping into the pond, we have,

> In the day, they ask for dark;
> in the night, for dawn:
> the cries of frogs.
> — Buson

and,

> With an air of perfect composure,
> it stares at the mountain:
> the frog.
> — Buson

And, as always, even the most mundane situations did not pass by unobserved,

> A dark night,
> and I'm drunk;
> but I'm not stepping on any toads.
> — Santoka

Summer Haiku

With just one sneeze
the summer
begins.

嚔一つに夏の明けり
Kusame hitotsu ni natsu no akeri
— Sakurai Shou

A bright day in May;
the sound of clippers
snipping a rose.

薔薇を剪る鋏刀の音や五月晴
Bara wo kiru hasami no oto ya satsukibare
— Shiki

When they scatter,
they do not rely on the wind;
poppy flowers.

散る時は風も頼まずけしの花
Chiru toki wa kaze mo tanomazu keshi no hana
— Ochi Etsujin

Pomegranate flowers blooming
at the thatched door;
shower clouds.

草の戸柘榴花咲夕立雲
Kusa no to zakurobana saku yuudachigumo
— Iwamoto Bokugai

Early summer rain!
One night, secretly,
a moon through the pines.

五月雨やある夜ひそかに松の月
Samidare ya aru yo hisoka ni matsu no tsuki
— Oshima Ryota

In my begging bowl.
tomorrow's rice;
a cool evening breeze.

鉄鉢に明日の米あり夕涼み
Teppatsu ni asu no kome ari yuu suzumi
— Ryokan

All hale and hearty,
squash flowers,
too.

みんなたつしやでかぼちやのはなも
Minna tassha de kabocha no hana mo
— Santoka

Light spilling
from their bodies;
summer insects.

夏虫の身よりこぼるる光哉

Natsumushi no mi yori koboruru hikari kana

— Moro Nanimaru

In this world.
no matter what,
there are butterflies.

世の中や蝶々とまれかくもあれ

Yo no naka ya chocho tomare kakumo are

— Nishiyama Soin

In the growth of grass,
the baseball lanes
are white.

草茂みベースボールの道白し

Kusa shigemi besuboru no michi shiroshi

— Shiki

Rainy season mist;
in the mountain hot spring,
daytime lamps.

梅雨霧や山の温泉宿の昼ランプ

Tsuyugiri ya yama no onsenyado no hiru ranpu

— Tanaka Bisui

Milk vetch;
I, too, was once
a child.

蓮華草我も一度は子供なり

Rengeso ware mo ichido wa kodomo nari

— Shiki

A continuing cloud
of paulownia flowers;
coming twilight.

桐の花くもりつづけてくれにけり

Kiri no hana kumori tsuzukete kure ni keri

— Miyamoto Koken

In the dark garden,
in the hushed night,
a peony.

園くらき夜を静かなる牡丹かな

Sono kuraki yo wo shizuka naru botan kana

— Kaya Shirao

The lights of fireflies,
warmth for the insects
in the fields.

蛍火は野中のむしの炙かな

Hotarubi wa nonaka no mushi no aburu kana

— Haruzumi

The kingfisher;
shining on its soaked feathers,
the setting sun.

翡翠やぬれ羽にうつる夕日影
Kawasemi ya nureha ni utsuru yuuhikage
— Tori

Worn down on a journey
sick and thin;
setting out mosquito smudge.

旅疲れと病ひやつれに蚊遣して
Tabitsukare to yamai yatsure ni kayari shite
— Shiki

Just when
everyone wants to nap,
a reed warbler.

人のみなねぶたき時のぎようぎようし
Hito no mina nebutaki toki no gyogyoshi
— Ryokan

A short night;
a mother and child
taking a nap.

短夜は子にそふ母の昼寝かな
Mijikayo wa ko ni sou haha no hirune kana
— Haga Issho

Peeing
on the lotus leaves;
the acolyte.

蓮の葉に小便すれば御舎利かな
Hasu no ha ni shoben sureba ojari kana
— Tokabo Shikou

An evening shower;
ducks run around the house
quacking.

白雨や家を回りて家鴨なく
Shirasame ya ie wo megurite ahiru naku
— Enomoto Kikaku

A short night;
people talking
on the second floor.

短夜の人話し居る二階かな
Mijikayo no hito hanashi iru nikai kana
— Yagasaki Kiho

Summer sake
riding along with me on the way
to being broke.

夏酒やわれと乗りこむ火の車
Natsuzake ya ware to norikomu hi no kuruma
— Mako Hokushi

The birds far off;
    on the handrail,
  peonies.

とり遠うして高欄に牡丹かな
Tori tou shite koran ni botan kana
— Oshima Ryota

Looking at the terraced
    green rice fields
  from the mountain pass.

峠から見る段々の青田かな
Toge kara miru dandan no aota kana
— Shiki

Butterflies,
    from back to front,
  fluttering.

てふてふうらからおもてへひらひら
Chocho ura kara omote e hirahira
— Santoka

Fireflies seen in the evening;
  somewhere,
  a watery moon.

宵に見しほたるやいづこ水の月
Yoi ni mishi hotaru ya izuko mizu no tsuki
— Kaya Shirao

Approaching the bamboo;
in a scattered rain,
fireflies.

竹に来て乱るる雨のほたるかな
Take ni kite midaruru ame no hotaru kana
— Tsukamatsu Roko

Neither hand aware
of the other, fingertips
picking bracken.

右ひだりしれぬ蕨の手先かな
Migi hidari shirenu warabi no tesaki kana
— Mitsujo

Bush clover and pampas grass,
be my guides
on the way I go.

萩すすきわが行く道のしるべせよ
Hagi susuki waga yuku michi no shirube se yo
— Ryokan

At the verge of a swarm
of mosquitoes, a dim
three day moon.

蚊ばしらのきはほのぼのとみつかの月
Kabashira no kiwa honobono to mikka no tsuki
— Mako Bokudo

Irises and me,
drunk
at this cottage.

かきつばた我れこの亭に酔ひにけり
Kakitsubata ware kono tei ni yoinikeri
— Ryokan

Passing by an unseen house;
smoke
of mosquito smudge.

隠れ家にすぎた蚊遣のけぶりかな
Kakurega ni sugita kayari no keburi kana
— Hakuba Sanjin

Inside the mosquito netting,
forgetting for a while
being in this world.

世の中をしばし忘れて蚊屋の中
Yo no naka wo shibashi wasurete kaya no naka
— Hasebe Ryukyo

Mixed in with the sound
of scrubbing the pot,
frogs in the rain.

なべみがくおとにまぎるる雨蛙
Nabe migaku oto ni magiruru amegaeru
— Ryokan

A sudden shower;
being resigned
out in the fields.

ゆふだちに思ひ切つたる野中かな

Yudachi ni omoikittaru nonaka kana

— Shirai Chosui

A night of conversations:
the chirping
of insects.

吪さるる夜とは成りけり虫のこゑ

Hanasaruru yo to wa narikeri mushi no koe

— Tenryo

Behind the shelf
for wooden clogs,
a chirping cricket.

下駄箱の奥になきけりきりぎりす

Getabako no oku ni nakikeri kirigirisu

— Shiki

Of the house where I was born,
no traces;
fireflies.

うまれた家はあとかたもないほうたる

Umaretaru ie wa atokata mo nai hotaru

— Santoka

Hearing the toad,
     my ears were cleansed;
the rain clearing.

蟇を聞く耳澄めば雨のやみゐたり
Hiki wo kiku mimi sumeba ame no yamiitari

— Tanaka Bisui

A large ant
     crossing the straw floor;
the heat!

大蟻のたたみをありくあつさ哉
Oo'ari no tatami wo ariku atsusa kana

— Fujimori Sobaku

A shame this place
     has no name;
the mountain cherries!

名の付かぬ所かはゆし山桜
Na no tsukanu tokoro kawayushi yamazakura

— Koshun

Japanese pinks,
     seeds falling on a plain
of summer fields.

撫子や夏野の原の落し種
Nadeshiko ya natsuno no hara otoshidane

— Sogi Hoshi

The child on my back
     playing with my hair;
the heat!

負うた子に髪なぶらるる暑さかな
Outa ko ni kami naburaruru atsusa kana

— Ichu

While silently
     reading the sutra, morning glories
blooming.

看経の間を朝顔の盛りかな
Kankin no ma wo asagao no sakari kana

— Morikawa Kyoriku

The morning glory,
     day by day creating
flowers.

朝顔やその日その日の花の出来
Asagao ya sono hi sono hi no hana no deki

— Koiya Sanpu

When told,
     "You lost weight this summer,"
I answer with tears.

夏瘦と人にこたふる泪かな
Natsuyase to hito ni kota'uru namida kana

— Yujodan

Inviting the storm
　　into the deep mountains:
the cuckoo's call.

顔鳥や深山あらしをさそふこゑ
Kaodori ya miyama arashi wo sasou koe

— Inei Teijo

Going out to the gate,
　　the cool air
scolds my house.

門へ出てわが家をそしる涼みかな
Kado e dete waga ya wo soshiru suzumi kana

— Genbu Bo

Cutting bamboo at night;
　　the sounds of mosquitoes,
far away.

竹切つて蚊の声遠き夕かな
Take kitte ka no koe touki yuu kana

— Kaya Shirao

My upbringing:
　　bathing in a deep blue lake
in perennial summer.

常夏の碧き湖あびわがそだつ
Tokonatsu no aoki umi abi waga sodatsu

— Sugita Hisajo

The bird that caught my eye
disappears
in the peaks of the clouds.

目にさはtる鳥は消えたり曇の嶺
Me ni sawaru tori wa kietari kumo no mine

— Fukuda Chiyo-ni

Waking up without a man;
how scary inside
the mosquito netting.

男なき寝覚はこはい蚊帳かな
Otoko naki nezame wa kowai kacho kana

— Yujodan

Chased by a snake.
How can I go home
from here?

蛇に追はれて何地かへるらん
Kuchinawa ni owarete izuchi kaeruran

— Yamazaki Sokan

Running water,
evening purification
of sweat and dust.

行水や汗も埃も夕祓
Gyozui ya ase mo hokori mo yuubarai

— Rosui

Not a single post
    where dragonflies
don't alight.

蜻蛉のとまらぬ杭はなかりけり
Tonbo no tomaranu kui wa nakarikeri

— Uehara Sansen

The fan stops
    and becomes
    an ugly machine.

扇風機止り醜き機械となれり
Senpuki tomari minikuki kikai to nareri

— Usuda Aro

When beaten, it disgorges
    daytime mosquitoes,
    the wooden temple drum.

叩かれて昼の蚊を吐く木魚かな
Tatakarete hiru no ka wo haku mokugyo kana

— Natsume Soseki

Going out to the lavatory;
    when I look,
    fireflies.

雪隠へ行かと見れば蛍かな
Setchin e yukado mireba hotaru kana

— Zaishiki

Morning glories!
    Beginning to get cloudy,
the market sky.

朝顔や濁り初めたる市の空
Asagao ya nigori hajimetaru ichi no sora
— Sugita Hisajo

Evening glories;
    flying around them,
moths at dusk.

夕顔を蛾のとびめぐる薄暮かな
Yuugao wo ga no tobimeguru hakubo kana
— Sugita Hisajo

Wakened by fleas;
    a hazy moon, but the clear cries
of an owl.

蚤に起きし靄の月まざと梟鳴く
Nomi ni okishi moya no tsuki maza to fukuro naku
— Hekigodo

Chased away,
    fireflies hidden
by the moon.

追はれては月にかくるるほたるかな
Owarete wa tsuki ni kakururu hotaru kana
— Oshima Ryota

An old pond,
a frog jumps in;
the sound of water.

古池や蛙飛び込む水の音
Furu'ike ya kawazu tobikomu mizu no oto
— Basho

A new pond,
a frog jumps in;
no sound at all.

新池やかはづとびこむ音もなし
Ara'ike ya kawazu tobikomu oto mo nashi
— Ryokan

Though the bright sun shines
relentlessly, still,
an autumnal wind.

あかあかと日はつれなくも秋の風
Aka aka to hi wa tsurenaku mo aki no kaze
— Basho

Autumn

秋は山が粧う
In the Autumn, the Mountains Adorn Themselves

With autumn comes relief from the cumbrous heat of summer, and haiku poets employ a number of *kigo*, or season words, to describe the new coolness, the morning cold, the night chill, and the new clarity of the air,

> Morning cold;
> > the young monk recites the sutra
> in a bright, clear voice.
> > > — Shiki

Autumn brings clear days and bright moons, but is also a time of unexpected showers,

> Autumnal showers off and on,
> > even so, how warm
> my hermitage.
> > > — Seigetsu

> Autumnal rains.
> > In this way it gets colder
> and colder.
> > > — Takahama Kyoshi

This is the season for harvesting rice—the principal food of the Japanese—and the concomitant scarecrows keep away other unwanted "harvesters." Harvest season also sees the making of rice straw goods such as raincoats and sandals,

> Silently putting them on:
> > today's
> straw sandals.
> > > — Santoka

In the past, pilgrimages and walking journeys were popular at this time of year, thanks in no small part to the beautiful autumnal leaves, the bright orange persimmons that decorate the countryside, or the fallen chestnuts scattered on the mountain paths. One of the favorite walks taken by the haiku poets was the Kiso Road, which runs through a mountainous area of central Japan, and the name of the road became a sort of motif for autumn itself,

> Horse chestnuts of the Kiso;
> souvenirs for those
> of this floating world.
>
> — Basho

> Flowing right in
> to the Kiso Mountains:
> the Milky Way.
>
> — Issa

Various animals are abundant during the autumnal season, and the naming of them in a haiku is meant to show the poet's grasp of the moment. The loneliness of the solitary deer, the seasonal fish put on the tables, the flocks of birds migrating to the south, and of course, the little sparrows that share part of the rice crops and keep the poets company even when the weather turns cold. But it may be surprising to us, fundamentally an indoor people, how much the local insects touch the hearts of the haiku writers—crickets, dragonflies, the remaining flies, worms, and especially the cicadas, whose cries of *mi, mi, mi* fill the forests and woods around temples and shrines. These cries are particularly poignant, as they mark the insects last days of life after breaking out of their protective shells,

> May at least one of them
> remain alive:
> autumn cicadas.
>
> — Yayu

The silence:
    penetrating the rocks,
  the cries of the cicadas.

    — Basho

Finally, the autumn season brings with it a time of solitude and self-reflection. Even as the mountains adorn themselves with the colorful leaves of the trees, the traveling poet is alone, with a unique perspective and vision,

On this road
    no one goes;
  dusk in autumn.

    — Basho

Autumn Haiku

Painting flowering plants
every day;
autumn begins.

草花を描く日課や秋に入る
Kusabana wo egaku nikka ya aki ni iru
— Shiki

A sneeze
confirms it:
autumn has come.

秋来ぬと合点させたる嚏かな
Aki kinu to gaten sasetaru kusame kana
— Buson

My summer sash
shriveled by the wind
this morning of autumn.

夏帯や風に縮る今朝の秋
Natsuobi ya kaze ni chijikeru kesa no aki
— Zaishiki

Pleasantly drunk;
falling
leaves.

ほろほろ酔うて木の葉ふる
Horohoro youte konoha furu

— Santoka

Children of the gods
running after them here and there;
falling autumn leaves.

神の子のあちこちと追ふや散る紅葉
Kami no ko no achikochi to ou ya chiru momiji

— Shiki

The morning glory
at the tip of a tendril
arrives at autumn.

朝顔のつるさき秋に届きけり
Asagao no tsurusaki aki ni todokikeri

— Shiki

Arranging bellflowers;
for a time,
a temporary study.

桔梗活けてしばらく仮の書斎哉
Kikyo ikete shibaraku kari no shosai kana

— Shiki

Thinking I had no need
to swat it,
the autumn fly.

うたずともよかったものを秋の蠅
Utazu tomo yokkata mono wo aki no hae

— Fugo

A full moon;
in the midst of the pampas grass,
a single house.

名月や芒の中の一軒家
Meigetsu ya susuki no naka no ikken-ya

— Iwamoto Bokugai

Fine weather;
a single butterfly sipping
from a chrysanthemum.

蝶ひとつ菊に喰入日和かな
Cho hitotsu kiku ni ku'iru hiyori kana

— Oshima Ryota

Night sinks deeper,
deeper, late autumn rains
falling.

沈み行く夜の底へ底へ時雨落つ
Shizumiyuku yo no soko e soko e shigure otsu

— Santoka

Thinking up
    sublime verses, at night,
  an autumnal blast.

雄大な句を思ふ夜の野分かな
Yudai na ku wo omou yo no nowaki kana

— Ito Shou

Lightning strikes,
    entering my thoughts;
  at night on a journey.

稲妻の懐に入る旅寝かな
Inazuma no futokoro ni iru tabine kana

— Sakurai Shou

Passing through autumn,
    abandoned by its leaves:
  Japanese holly.

秋経るや葉にすてられて梅もどき
Aki heru ya ha ni suterarete umemodoki

— Seigetsu

All night long,
    listening to the autumn wind;
  the mountains out back.

終宵秋風聞やうらの山
Yomosugara akikaze kiku ya ura no yama

— Sora

Walking the Kiso Road,
I, too, a traveler;
falling leaves of the tree.

木曾路ゆく我れも旅人散る木の葉

Kisoji yuku ware mo tabibito chiru ko no ha

— Usuda Aro

Looking like
lightning;
a shooting star.

稲妻のおもかげ見てや夜這星

Inazuma no omokage mite ya yobaiboshi

— Kaedei Ryotoku

At some point,
in a great hurry, the sky
turned to autumn.

大旱のいつしか空は秋となり

Taiso no itsushika sora ha aki to nari

— Sakurai Do'on

Standing alone,
bathed from head to toe
by the autumn wind.

摩頂してひとりたちけり秋のかぜ

Macho shite hitori tachikeri aki no kaze

— Ryokan

A dog barking,
 nobody home;
  red-tinged ivy.

犬吠えて家に人なし蔦紅葉

Inu hoete ie ni hito nashi tsutamomiji

— Ikenishi Gonsui

No place to throw away
 the bath water;
  the cries of insects.

行水の捨てどころなし虫の声

Gyozui no sutedokoro nashi mushi no koe

— Ueshima Onitsura

After their chirping,
 it's a bit lonesome;
  autumn cicadas.

鳴くあとのやや寂しさや秋の蝉

Naku ato no yaya samishisa ya aki no semi

— Shiki

Removing the shutters,
 a sight of autumn:
  the confusion of lamp lights.

雨戸こす秋の姿や灯の狂ひ

Amado kosu aki no sugata ya hi no kurui

— Yoshihira

Billowing clouds, my journey, too,
has come to an end;
I buy tobacco.

鰯雲旅も終りの煙草買ふ

Iwashigumo tabi mo owari no tabako kau

— Rokugawa Suisei

Lightning!
Yesterday in the east,
today in the west.

稲妻や昨日は東けふは西

Inazuma ya kinou wa higashi kyou wa nishi

— Enomoto Kikaku

How delightful!
Fallen leaves
in the unswept garden.

不掃除の庭に嬉しき落葉哉

Fusoji no niwa ni ureshiki rakuyo kana

— Zaishiki

Late autumn rain;
when I run inside
it clears up.

時雨けり走り入りけり晴れにけり

Shigurekeri hashiri irikeri harenikeri

— Izen Bo

The voices of birds
    disappearing one by one;
autumnal mist.

声々に鳥は消えて霞かな
Koegoe ni tori wa kiete kasumi kana

— Miyamoto Koken

Not seeing the signs
    that they will soon die;
    the cries of cicadas.

やがて死ぬ気色は見えず蝉の声
Yagate shinu keshiki wa miezu semi no koe

— Rito

Autumn is coming,
    not only
    in the wind.

来る秋は風ばかりでもなかりけり
Kuru aki wa kaze bakari demo nakarikeri

— Mako Hokushi

No smell
    of cows or horses;
    late autumn rains.

牛馬の臭みもなくて時雨かな
Ushi uma no kusami mo nakute shigure kana

— So Roka

A mountain village;
through the wide doorway,
the village in autumn.

山里や戸口のひろき里の秋
Yamazato ya toguchi no hiroki sato no aki
— Kurada Kassan

A multitude of hands
is too much;
catching fireflies.

大勢の手にあまりたる蛍かな
Taisei no te ni amaritaru hotaru kana
— Ryoto

Departing autumn
roads
of fallen red leaves.

行秋を道々こぼす紅葉かな
Yuku akiwo michimichi kobosu momiji kana
— Nakagawa Otsuyu

In the cemetery,
autumn fireflies;
two or three.

墓原や秋の蛍のふたつみつ
Tsukahara ya aki no hotaru no futatsu mitsu
— Kato Gensho

Spreading vinegar
on my old gums;
the autumn wind.

酢のしみる老の歯茎や秋の風
Su no shimiru oi no haguki ya aki no kaze
— Nakamura Hakusen

Catching dragonflies;
today, how far
has he gone?

蜻蛉釣今日はどこまで行つたやら
Tonbogari kyo wa doko made itta yara
— Fukuda Chiyo-ni

There are human voices
in the grasses and trees, too:
an autumnal blast.

草も木も人の声ある野分かな
Kusa mo ki mo hito no koe aru nowaki kana
— Yamaguchi Rajin

Coming to chase away
despair:
autumn cicadas.

うきこと追はえ来るなり秋の蝉
Ukikoto owaekuru nari aki no semi
— Ginkado Banzan

A day of mist;
in the evening mountain's shadow,
the candy vendor's flute.

かすむ日や夕山かげの飴の笛
Kasumu hi ya yuuyama kage no ame no fue

— Issa

People's voices
in the endless
autumn night.

人声に尾のなき秋の夕べかな
Hitogoe ni o no naki aki no yuube kana

— Takamura Wagyu

At night, a late autumn rain;
the sound of an umbrella
going in next door.

小夜時雨隣へはひる傘の音
Sayo shigure tonari e hairu kasa no oto

— Matsukura Ranran

In the oil lamp,
mosquitoes cry and fall;
night deepens.

油火に蚊の鳴落て夜更けたり
Aburabi ni ka no naki'ochite yo fuketari

— Nakamura Hakusen

Pampas grass scattered
by the nighttime
autumn wind.

秋風に芒打ちちる夕べかな
Akikaze ni susuki uchichiru yuube kana
— Guji Nojun

Autumn, the dream, cleansing the grime
of the floating world
in a morning bath.

秋や夢浮世の垢を明日の湯
Aki ya yume ukiyo no aka wo ashita no yu
— Zaishiki

Clouds going up,
clouds coming down;
the autumn sky.

上ゆくと下来る曇や秋の空
Ue yuku to shita kuru kumo ya aki no sora
— Sogyaku Bonsho

Enveloping
the people of the town;
chirping cicadas.

市中の人をまとふ蝉の声
Ichinaka no hito wo matou semi no koe
— Koshigaya Gozan

My bamboo hat now baggage;
away from home,
the autumn chill.

笠を荷にする旅空や秋の冷
Kasa wo ni ni suru tabizora ya aki no hie

— Seigetsu

Going right along,
lightning striking
through the Kiso Valley.

いなづまのぶつかり行くや木曾の谷
Inazuma no butsukari yuku ya Kiso no tani

— Tsukamatsu Roko

The crags of Kiso Valley;
the sinking
autumn sun.

木曾谷の岩が根しづむ秋日かな
Kisodani no iwagane shizumu aki-hi kana

— Hosha

Making a face
as though thinking nothing at all;
late autumn.

思ふことなき顔しても秋のくれ
Omou koto naki kao shite mo aki no kure

— Sutejo

On the autumn plateau
    all the butterflies I see:
        yellow butterflies.

高原の秋や逢ふ蝶見皆黄蝶
Takahara no aki ya au cho mina kicho
    — Morozumi Chikushuro

Going out at dawn,
        going out at dusk,
    the autumn wind.

朝出れば夕暮出れば秋の風
Asa dereba yuugure dereba aki no kaze
    — Nakamura Hakusen

As though gazing at heaven and earth,
        chrysanthemums
    in the rain.

天地の眼るが如し雨の菊
Tenchi no miru ga gotoshi ame no kiku
    — Tsukamatsu Roko

Know what is enough;
        the butterfly's dew
    on the flower.

たる事を知るや胡蝶の花の露
Taru koto wo shiru ya kocho no hana no tsuyu
    — Haiso Gitoku

Leaving the mountain path,
bush clover and pampas grass;
my heavy rain hat.

萩すすき山路を出る笠おもし

Hagi susuki yamaji wo izuru kasa omoshi

— Chinejo

Even while
cooking clams;
the autumn cold.

蛤を焚くにつけても秋寒し

Hamaguri wo yaku ni tsukete mo aki samushi

— Sakurai Shou

Burning fallen leaves,
day after day,
a miserable hearth.

落葉日々焚いて炉浅くなりにけり

Ochiba hibi taite ro asaku narinikeri

— Shimada Kumanji

Heavily on the collar
of my hemp garment,
the swash of bush clover.

かたびらの襟には重し萩の音

Katabira no eri ni wa omoshi hagi no oto

— Fukuda Chiyo-ni

The evening cicada abruptly chirps,
just once;
a moonlit night.

ひぐらしのふいと一聲月夜かな
Higurashi no fui to hitogoe tsukiyo kana

— Hajin

The mountain reflected
in clear skies,
withered pampas grass.

青空に山のうつるや枯尾花
Aozora ni yama no utsuru y kareobana

— Sakurai Shou

Who can remain hardened
with the pathos
of fleeting autumn?

ゆく秋のあはれを誰にかたらまし
Yuku aki no aware wo dare ni kataramashi

— Ryokan

The seed of an afternoon nap
for all:
an autumn moon.

皆人の昼寝の種や秋の月
Minahito no hirune no tane ya aki no tsuki

— Matsunaga Teitoku

Eating my rice
in loneliness;
late autumn.

淋しさに飯をくふ也秋の暮
Sabishisa ni kome wo kuu nari aki no kure
— Issa

Well then, I, too,
should go home now;
this autumn eve.

いざさらば我も返らんあきの暮
Izasaraba ware mo kaeruran aki no kure
— Ryokan

A crow perches
on a withered branch;
the end of autumn.

枯枝に烏の止りけり秋の暮
Kare'eda ni karasu no tomarikeri aki no kure
— Basho

Winter

冬は山が寝る
In the Winter, the Mountains Sleep

With the short days, long nights, and the rice fields and mountains covered in snow, winter is a time for withdrawing inside for much of Japan. Of course, there are outdoor activities for children—making snowmen and throwing snowballs at each other—but by and large, it has traditionally been a time for "winter seclusion," when families gathered around the hearth amusing themselves as they could,

> Showing everyone I got the answer
> to the riddle,
> winter seclusion.
> — Shiki

or recluses trying to stay warm in their tiny hermitages,

> Boiling daikon:
> dinner together
> with the children.
> — Hekigodo

> Holding my hands
> over a hibachi
> without a flame.
> — Ozaki Hosai

> Morning and night,
> my debt to the radish;
> winter seclusion.
> — Seigetsu

Despite the difficulties that this time of year may bring, there is a strong poetical attraction to the beauty of the winter season, which is expressed by descriptions of the first snow, the winter moon, and references to all the plants that still bloom—tea flowers, plum blossoms and "cold chrysanthemums," to name but a few. Even the withered moors are seen with the eye of poetry,

On the way,
the day grows dark;
the withered moor.

— Mokudo

And, finding significance where others might not,

The important priest
empties his bowels
on the withered moor.

— Buson

Wildlife seems to be left only to the birds that remain on the Japanese archipelago, and among these are ducks, plovers, wrens and the ubiquitous and beloved sparrows,

Softly falling snow;
the warmheartedness
of little birds.

— Santoka

Winter rains;
playing with sparrows
for half the day.

— Tsukamatsu Roko

Food, and the availability thereof, was historically a matter of concern to everyone during the bleak winter months, and haiku poets were no exception. Seafood has always been a staple in this season, including yellowtail, carp, blowfish (which if prepared incorrectly could be fatal) and oysters. Perhaps the most unimaginable of such winter fare for Western readers is the *namako*, or sea slug. Eaten for good health, this ocean creature can be kept alive in buckets even in cold climates, and served in small slices as a delicacy. Its strange appearance, even to the poet, has not gone unnoticed,

> Is that its head or its tail?
> I'm not sure.
> The sea slug.
>
> — Kyorai

Winter was necessarily a time of less activity, yet no action was too insignificant to go unnoticed and put into verse,

> Just for a moment
> the kitten holds down
> a fallen leaf.
>
> — Issa

Winter Haiku

First snow;
    the morning glory asks
for yet another morning.

初雪や朝顔は翌の頼みあり
Hatsuyuki ya asagao wa asu no tanomi ari
— Kato Gensho

Falling on this world,
    again, a lodging
in early winter rain.

世にふるはさらに時雨の宿りかな
Yo ni furu wa sara ni shigure no yadori kana
— Sogi Hoshi

Hey, now, cricket,
    be quiet for a while;
first winter rain.

やあしばらく蟋だまれ初時雨
Yaa shibaraku korogi damare hatsushigure
— Issa

Watching the first snow
  on faraway mountains,
in fine weather.

遠山の初雪見する日和かな

Tou yama no hatsuyuki mi suru hiyori kana

— Seigetsu

The light of early winter rain,
  suddenly
on my sleeping mat.

寝筵にさつと時雨の明り哉

Nemushiro ni satto shigure no akari kana

— Issa

In Ogiso, a woman
  playing in the first snow;
disheveled hair.

小木曾女や初雪たわむ額髪

Ogisome ya hatsuyuki tawamu hitaigami

— Fujimori Sobaku

Winter is coming,
  perched on a scarecrow,
a crow!

冬来て案山子にとまる烏かな

Fuyu kite kakashi ni tomaru karasu kana

— Enomoto Kikaku

My hermitage not much
more than an umbrella;
early winter rain.

笠程な庵とおもへ初時雨
Kasa hodo na iori to omoe hatsushigure
— Takebe Ryotai

Village after village, a light brown
veiled in mist
early winter.

村々は茶色に霞む小春かな
Muramura wa chairo ni kasumu koharu kana
— Takebe Ryotai

Even no water birds
to be seen,
crossing the inlet; the cold!

水鳥も見えぬ江わたる寒かな
Mizutori mo mienu e wataru samusa kana
— Buson

Leaving the house,
a winter moon
on white walls.

家出る冬月の白壁
Ie deru togetsu no shirakabe
— Sumiyama Kyuji

Opening the door,
      the glare of snow all the way
to the hearth.

戸のあいて雪のまばゆさ炉端まで
To no aite yuki no mabayusa robata made

— Morozumi Chikushuro

Night at the end of the year;
      a cold bed,
just one.

師走の夜のつめたい寝床一つあるきり
Shiwasu no yo no tsumetai nedoko hitotsu arukiri

— Ozaki Hosai

A snowy day
      but still someone's child
is filling the tub.

雪の日やあれも人の子樽ひろひ
Yuki no hi ya aremo hito no ko taru hiroi

— Nishijima Tsuma

In the cold,
      I abandoned the broom
under a pine tree.

つめたさに箒捨てけり松の下
Tsumetasa ni hoki sutekeri matsu no shita

— Taigi

An ancient village,
       frost clearing up;
       the sound of bamboo.

古里や霜明けかかる竹の声

Furusato ya shimo akekakaru take no koe

— Sakurai Shou

My appearance
       also pathetic;
       the dreary moor.

我形も哀れに見ゆる枯野かな

Waga nari mo aware ni miyuru kareno kana

— Chigetsu

Puffins
       gathering in the north wind
       and flying away.

海雀を北風に群れしめ解らんす

Kaijaku wo kita kaze ni mureshime kairan su

— Hashimoto Takako

The desolation of winter;
       small birds foraging
       in the leek field.

冬されや小鳥のあさる韮畑

Fuyuzare ya kotori no asaru nirabatake

— Buson

On the snowy plain,
Jizo's offerings?
Sparrows.

雪野の地蔵尊に供物がある雀ら

Yukino no Jizo-son ni kumotsu ga aru suzumera

— Sumiyama Kyuji

A calming sea,
the sound of the stonecutter;
falling hail.

海静かなるに石切る音や霰降る

Umi shizuka naru ni ishikiru oto ya arare furu

— Hekigodo

The loneliness of winter;
walking through a small village,
dogs barking.

冬ざれの小村を行けば犬吠ゆる

Fuyuzareno komura wo yukeba inu hoyuru

— Shiki

Thin snow falling
but still the scent of flowers
in the tearoom.

淡雪のふるも茶湯の花香かな

Awayuki no furu mo chanoyu no hanaka kana

— Kawakami Fuhaku

Winter seclusion,
  even the insects go respectfully
underground.

冬ごもり虫螻までも穴かこし

Fuyugomori mushikera made mo anakakoshi

  — Matsunaga Teitoku

Well then, this is it:
  at last, my dwelling?
Five feet of snow.

これがまあつひの栖か雪五尺

Kore ga maa tsui no sumika ka yuki goshaku

  — Issa

Sake,
  my health drink!
Winter seclusion.

酒といふ延齢丹や冬籠

Sake to iu enreitan ya fuyugomori

  — Seigetsu

A winter shower;
  the hidden sad croaking
of a toad.

夕時雨蟇ひそみ音に愁ふ哉

Yuu shigure gama hisomine ni ureu kana

  — Buson

Night after night,
    going in the same direction
  chanting the Nembutsu in the cold.

夜や夜や同じ方行く寒念仏

Yo ya yo ya onaji ho yuku kannembutsu

— Yagasaki Kiho

In the cold, the sound of the Nembutsu;
    solemnly entering
  through the gate.

寒念仏声おごそかに門に入る

Kannembutsu koe ogosoka ni kado ni iru

— Iwamoto Bokugai

Just when I remembered
    the name of the mountain,
  it started to snow.

山の名を覚えし頃雪来り

Yama no na wo oboeshi koro yuki kitari

— Takahama Kyoshi

Clouds coming and going,
    how many times?
  Returning winter rains.

曇の往来のいく度か時雨返すなり

Kumo no orai no ikutabi ka shigure kaesu nari

— Shimada Kumanji

A winter storm;
　　the sound of water
　bursting over the crags.

こがらしや岩に裂行水の声

Kogarashi ya iwa ni sakeyuku mizu no koe

— Buson

Watching a beggar
　　scolding a child,
　a wintry moon.

子を叱る乞食見たりや冬の月

Ko wo shikaru kojiki mitari ya fuyu no tsuki

— Iwamoto Bokugai

Today, too,
　　beneath the dwindling snow storm,
　a perfectly round sun.

今日も暮るる吹雪の底の大日輪

Kyo mo kururu fubuki no soko no dainichirin

— Usuda Aro

A day of snow;
　　a chilly reception from folks
　in my home town.

雪の日や古郷人のぶあしらひ

Yuki no hi ya kokyobito no bu'ashirai

— Issa

I'd even forgotten
it was falling;
the quiet of snow.

降るをさへわするる雪のしづかさよ

Furu wo sae wasururu yuki no shizukasa yo

— Fujimori Sobaku

Nothing moving
in the mountains or fields;
a morning of snow.

野に山に動くものなし雪の朝

No ni yama ni ugoku mono nashi yuki no asa

— Fukuda Chiyo-ni

Lonely on cold nights
in Kiso;
getting old.

膝頭木曾の夜寒に古びけり

Hizagashira kiso no yokan ni furubi keri

— Issa

A morning moon
like a dream; Kiso
in deep snow.

夢のよな朝月木曾は雪深く

Yume no yona asa tsuki Kiso wa yuki fukaku

— Tanaka Bisui

The path to the nunnery;
only rape blossoms
falling.

尼寺よただ菜の花の散る径
Amadera yo tada nanohana no chiru komichi

— Ikenishi Gonsui

No matter how you look at it,
there is nothing quite as mysterious
as snow.

なんと見ても雪ほど玄き物はなし
Nan to mite mo yuki hodo kuroki mono wa nashi

— Saito Tokugen

Night after night
stepping through snow,
the journey, half over.

宵々に雪踏む旅も半ばなり
Yoi yoi ni yuki fumu tabi mo nakaba nari

— Usuda Aro

From all directions,
morning,
sun shining on snow.

四方から日のさす雪のあした哉
Yomo kara hi no sasu yuki no ashita kana

— Fujimori Sobaku

Winter sparrows,
　　hopping down, hopping along
again and again.

とび下りて弾みやまずよ寒雀
Tobi'orite hazumi yamazuyo kansuzume

— Bosha

Opening the gate,
　　throwing out the tea husks:
a snowstorm.

門明けて茶のから捨る吹雪かな
Mon akete cha no kara suteru fubuki kana

— Fujimori Sobaku

A wintry wind;
　　in the city I hear
a koto player by trade.

木枯らしや市に業の琴をきく
Kogarashi ya ichi ni tatsuki koto wo kiku

— Kaya Shirao

A cool head and warm feet;
　　all wrapped up;
a snowy road.

頭寒足ねつう包むや雪の道
Zukansokunetsu utsutsumu ya yuki no michi

— Jiyo

How stately:
    the standing tree
in the wintry mountain.

冬立木いかめしや山のたた住居
Fuyu tachiki ikameshi ya yama no tatazumai
— Dansui

At the door the sound of the dog
    turning over in sleep;
    winter seclusion.

戸に犬の寝がへる音や冬籠
To ni inu no negaeru oto ya fuyugomori
— Buson

Lonely houses
    all in a row;
    the depth of winter.

さびしさの家ならびけり冬の奥
Sabishisa no ie narabikeri fuyu no oku
— Tsukamatsu Roko

Waking from sleep,
    I raise my head and look;
    the cold!

わがねたを首あげて見る寒さかな
Waga neta wo kubi agete miru samusa kana
— Yoshihira

The rocky crag;
　　mountain goats
in the winter sun.

岩はなや羚羊に冬の日ざし哉

Iwahana ya kamoshika ni fuyu no hizashi kana

— Nakamura Hakusen

Amidst moon and snow,
　　a place to leave
one's life.

月雪の中よ命の捨て所

Tsuki yuki no naka yo inochi no sutedokoro

— Ito Shou

A day of snow,
　　the color of the master seaman's
face.

雪の日や船頭どのの顔のいろ

Yuki no hi ya sendo dono no kao no iro

— Enomoto Kikaku

Off to buy sake
　　towards a crescent moon
in the winter rain.

しぐれへ三日月へ酒買ひに行く

Shigure e mikazuki e sake kai ni iku

— Santoka

A withering blast,
quickly dissipating;
the reflection of the moon.

木がらしや直におちつく水の月

Kogarashi ya jiki no ochitsuku mizu no tsuki

— Fukuda Chiyo-ni

How difficult turning over
at dawn;
the cold!

有明に振向きがたき寒さかな

Ariake ni furimukigataki samusa kana

— Naito Joso

Plum flowers:
red, red,
so red!

梅の花あかいは赤いはあかいはの

Ume no hana akai wa akai wa akai wa no

— Izen Bo

No sparrows creeping
through the hedge;
their tracks in the snow.

垣潜る雀ならなく雪の跡

Kaki kuguru suzume naranaku yuki no ato

— Yaba

The traveler eating a mandarin orange
as he goes;
the withered moor.

旅人の美柑くひ行く枯野哉
Tabibito no mikan kuiyuku kareno kana
— Shiki

The rustling sound
in the bamboo;
a night of snow.

さらさらと竹に音あり夜の雪
Sarasara to take ni oto ari yoru no yuki
— Shiki

Smelling my loincloth
out on a pole;
winter seclusion.

褌は竿にかがせつ冬ごもり
Fundoshi wa sao ni kagasetsu fuyugomori
— Keio Mokusetsu

Resigning myself,
I go outside to pee.
The cold!

身を捨てて小便に出る寒さかな
Mi wo sutete shoben ni deru samusa kana
— Genbu Bo

Half-heartedly
　　illuminating the clouds,
　a sad winter sky.

なまじひに曇照るさびし冬の空
Namajii ni kumo teru sabishi fuyu no sora
— Shimada Kumanji

A morning withering blast;
　　out on the ground, a crow
　calling.

木枯のけさは地に鳴くからすかな
Kogarashi no kesa wa chi ni naku karasu kana
— Watanabe Taisei

Solving the puzzle
　　and showing everyone;
　winter seclusion.

なぞなぞを解て見せりけり冬籠
Nazonazo wo toite miserikeri fuyugomori
— Shiki

Praise be the moonlit night,
　　praise be snow mixed with rain;
　beating the Buddhist bowl.

南無月夜南無雪時雨鉢叩
Namu tsukiyo namu yukishigure hachi tataki
— Inoue Shiro

New Year

元日登山
On New Year's, Climb a Mountain

In the West, we generally celebrate New Year's Eve with fireworks and the consumption of alcohol. These traditions are not ignored in Japan either,

> No shortcut
> to the sake shop;
> year's end.
> — Seigetsu

But for the Japanese and their poets, it is on the first day of the year, and the few days after, that the beginning of a new year is celebrated and observed. For the week before, families will prepare a special food for the visits of neighbors and colleagues, while on the first days of January, there are visits to local temples and shrines to pray for a good coming year,

> What I pray for
> is always the same;
> first visit to the shrine.
> — Takahama Kyoshi

There are also card games, battledore and shuttlecock, demonstrations of the ancient sport of *temari*, and contests of calligraphy for the young,

> How he stares at the orange;
> the prize
> for the first calligraphy of the year.
> — Issa

It is the "first" of almost everything, however, that is found interesting and significant for the few days after the first day itself:

Laughing and taking a deep breath;
getting used to the tub
for the first bath.

— Takahama Kyoshi

My first dream,
leaping over Mt. Fuji;
flowers and the moon.

— Kohaku

The first dream has traditionally been extraordinarily important. The most auspicious images are those of Mount Fuji, eggplants and falcons— eggplant because the word for this vegetable is *nasu*, a homonym for "accomplish" or "fulfill"; falcon because it flies so high, foretelling a promotion in rank, status or economic wellbeing; and Mount Fuji because it is the highest and most revered mountain in Japan.

There is another dream the Japanese traditionally hope to have on the first two nights of the New Year—that of the *takarabune* or treasure ship. This is a boat passengered by the Seven Lucky Gods, divinities originating in ancient Japan, China and India, representing longevity, prosperity, abundance, musical talent and so on. To have a such a dream was believed to indicate good fortune in the coming year, and sometimes people slept (and still sleep) with prints of the ship under their pillow to ensure having such a dream,

The treasure ship;
spreading it out
with an easy mind.

— Shinro

Such prints were sold on the street, often of poor quality:

How pathetic!
The men selling
treasure ships.

— Oemaru

Still, for just a cheap price, it was possible to buy great hope for the coming year.

Other New Year's motifs include the pine boughs that everyone puts on their gates or doors, the greeting cards sent out just as Westerners send Christmas cards, and the seven traditional herbs that are traditionally eaten on the seventh day of January to wish for good health.

For most, the fifth season is a time of renewal, goodwill toward one's neighbors, and a fresh look at the world. Or at least having that aspiration,

This is what I try to be:
a child
at New Year's.

— Issa

And,

First dawn of the New Year.
yesterday,
so far away.

— Ichiku

For the first of the year, it has traditionally been auspicious to view Mt. Fuji, even from a distance,

New Year's dawn;
let's take a look
at Mt. Fuji.

— Yamazaki Sokan

❧　❧　❧　❧　❧

New Year Haiku

Tomorrow is New Year's;
at least
I'll clip my nails.

あすは元日の爪でもきらう

Asu wa ganjitsu no tsume demo kiro

— Santoka

New Year's Eve:
things continuously withering
in the sound of the wind.

年の夜やものの枯れやまぬ風の音

Toshi no yo ya mono no kareyamanu kaze no oto

— Suiha

New Year's Eve:
something settled in this
unsettled world.

大晦日定めなき世の定めかな

Omisoka sadamenaki yo no sadame kana

— Ihara Saikaku

New Year's Eve;
the year's final scent:
early plum blossoms.

寒梅の薫りおさめや大三十日
Kanbai no kaori osame ya omisoka

— Shiki

How frightening!
A woman wearing glasses
at year's end.

恐しや女の眼鏡としの暮
Osoroshi ya onna no megane toshi no kure

— Ito Shintoku

Even the old folks
forget their cares;
year's end.

年寄もまぎれぬものや年の暮
Toshiyori mo magirenu mono ya toshi no kure

— Takeshita Ko'un

One full year,
tonight,
a cloud-covered moon.

ひととせの月を曇らす今宵かな
Hitotose no tsuki wo kumorasu koyoi kana

— Sogi Hoshi

Extinguishing the candles,
dawn is near;
New Year's Eve.

燭きつて暁ちかし大晦日
Shoku kitte akatsuki chikashi omisoka

— Natsume Soseki

Everything frivolous
has been said:
year's end.

軽薄をまをし尽して歳暮かな
Keihaku wo moshi tsukushite seibo kana

— Mako Bokudo

The New Year begins.
The wealth of my house?
A moon and starlit night.

年立や家中の富は星月夜
Toshitatsu ya yanaka no tomi wa hoshizukiyo

— Enomoto Kikaku

In my delight
I told it all;
my first dream of the year.

うれしさにはつ夢いふてしまひけり
Ureshisa ni hatsu'yume iute shimaikeri

— Shiki

My first dream!
I say nothing, keep it a secret,
and smile to myself.

初夢や秘めて語らず一人笑む

Hatsu yume ya himete katarazu hitori emu

— Sho-u

Was it a dream
at dawn? My thoughts
are hazy.

暁の夢かとぞ思ふ朧かな

Akatsuki no yume ka to zo omou oboro kana

— Natsume Soseki

Yes, I saw it,
but then forgot it:
the year's first dream.

初夢を見は見たりしが忘れけり

Hatsuyume wo mi wa mitarishi ga wasurekeri

— Ochi

My first dream was too good,
so they said
it was a lie.

あまりよき初夢うそと云れけり

Amari yoki hatsuyume uso to iwarekeri

— Takuchi

New Year's Day
    in my four-cornered
hut.

四角な庵の元日

Shikaku na iori no ganjitsu

— Ozaki Hosai

New Year's Day!
    Yesterday, how far away,
at dawn.

元日や昨日に遠き朝ぼらけ

Ganjitsu ya kino ni toki asaborake

— Ichiku

First day of the year;
    the color of the sky, too,
imbued with flowers.

空色も花と染めなす初日かな

Sora'iro mo ohana to somenasu hatsuhi kana

— Seigetsu

This morning
    it appears all the larger;
first sunrise.

今朝や猶大きく見ゆる初日の出

Kesa ya nao okiku miyuru hatsuhinode

— Wakaku

Washing my dirty
    hands and feet, I observe sunrise;
New Year's Day.

汚れたる手足を洗ひ初日見る
Yogoretaru te'ashi wo arai hatsuhi miru

— Morozumi Chikushuro

With or without
    New Year's;
      the scenery of Mt. Fuji!

富士の山師走ともなき景色かな
Fuji no yama shiwasu tomonaki keshiki kana

— Koshun

Clouds,
    drawn like a painting;
    first sunrise of the year.

画に書いたやうな曇あり初日の出
E ni kaita yo na kumo ari hatsuhinode

— Shusai

New Year's Day!
    And still, the sound of water
in the streams flowing through the fields.

元日やされば野川の水の音
Ganjitsu ya sareba nogawa no mizu no oto

— Yoshihira

The New Year begins,
this morning,
quietly, peacefully.

何事もなくて春たつあした哉

Nanigoto mo nakute haru tatsu ashita kana

— Inoue Shiro

A mountain hamlet,
the first sun is bowed to
about ten o'clock.

山里や初日を拝む十時頃

Yamazato ya hatsuhi wo ogamu juji goro

— Shiki

New Year's;
how novel:
dirt by the roadside!

道ばたの土めずらしやお正月

Michibata no tsuchi mezurashi ya o-shogatsu

— Issa

A New Year's greeting
to my temple;
first mist.

我院に御慶申さん初霞

Waga in ni gyokei mosan hatsugasumi

— Shofu-ni

New Year's Day!
Bright and clear;
sparrows conversing.

元日や晴れて雀の物語
Ganjitsu ya harete suzume no monogatari

— Retsujo

New Year's Day,
the Age of the Gods
brought to mind.

元日や神代の事も思はるる
Ganjitsu ya kamiyo no koto mo omowaruru

— Sogi Hoshi

My desire
is to always have the heart
of New Year's Day.

願わくは常も元日の心哉
Negawaku wa tsune mo ganjitsu no kokoro kana

— Wasei

The mind of New Year's
forever
like a baby's.

正月の心常ある赤子哉
Shogatsu no kokoro tsune aru akago kana

— Ichiryu

New Year's Day:
even the old
looks new.

元日や古き姿もあたらしき
Ganjitsu ya furuki sugata mo atarashiki
— Ginko

New Year's Day:
the beginning of harmony
of heaven and earth.

元日を天地和合の始哉
Ganjitsu wo tenchi wago no hajime kana
— Shiki

New Year's Day:
nothing good, nothing bad,
all of us human beings.

元日は是も非もなくて衆生なり
Ganjitsu wa ze mo hi mo nakute shujo nari
— Shiki

New Year's Day!
With what can you compare it?
The light of dawn.

元日や何に喩へん朝ぼらけ
Ganjitsu ya nani ni tatoen asaborake
— Kanno Tadatomo

New Year's Day:
    human nature,
      the root of a great tree.

元旦や大樹のもとの人ごころ

Gantan ya taiju no moto no hitogokoro

— Kaya Shirao

New Year's:
    a world of words,
    all frivolous.

正月言葉皆軽薄の世界哉

Shogatsu kotoba mina keihaku no sekai kana

— Mizon

This New Year,
    it's not that I have
    nothing in mind.

今年はと思ふことなきにしもあらず

Kotoshi wa to omou koto naki ni shimo arazu

— Shiki

New Year's Day!
    I bear no spite for those making footprints
in the snow.

元日や雪を踏む人憎からず

Ganjitsu ya yuki wo fumu hito nikukarazu

— Yayu

New Year's Day!
    Going inside the temple,
a bit lonely.

元日や寺にはいればものさびし

Ganjitsu ya tera ni haireba monosabishi

    — Hekigodo

New Year's Day:
    everyone starts bumbling
at their jobs.

元日の事皆非なるはじめかな

Ganjitsu no koto mina hi naru hajume kana

    — Takahama Kyoshi

Even on New Year's Day,
    travelers are seen
at the stable.

元日も旅人を見る駅かな

Ganjitsu mo tabibito wo miru umaya kana

    — Mizuma Sentoku

New Year's Day;
    people
passing by.

元日の人通りとはなりにけり

Ganjitsu no hitodori to wa narinikeri

    — Shiki

New Year's Day!
　　Dressed extravagantly;
　　eating my way to the poorhouse.

正月や着倒れの世を食ひたをれ
Shogatsu ya kidaore no yo wo kuidaore
　　　　　　—Tsukamatsu Roko

New Year's Day!
　　Throwing off my formal clothes,
　　I go out to play.

元日の袴脱ぎ捨て遊びけり
Ganjitsu no hakama nugisute asobikeri
　　　　— Hekigodo

Every face I see,
　　　without a care;
　　New Year's Day!

元日や誰貌見ても念のなき
Ganjitsu ya tagakao mite mo nen no naki
　　　　— Shigyoku

New Year's!
　　After three days,
　　people are old hat.

正月や三日過ぎれば人古し
Shogatsu ya mikka sugireba hito furushi
　　　　— Ranko

Same faces,
    same remarks;
New Year's Day.

同じ顔おなじ事いふ朝の春

Onaji kao onaji koto iu asa no haru

— Doraku

Spring has come,
    adding one foolishness
to another.

春立や愚の上に愚にかへる

Haru tatsu ya gu no ue ni gu ni kaeru

— Issa

The sound of water;
    the New Year
has arrived.

水音の、新年が来た

Mizu'oto no, shinnen ga kita

— Santoka

The first morning of spring;
    even my shadow
is healthy and hale.

影法師もまめ息災でけさの春

Kageboshi mo mame sokusai de kesa no haru

— Issa

New Year's!
    Even when the teetotaler comes,
  they offer sake.

正月や下戸の来てさへ酒を出す
Shogatsu ya geko no kite sae sake wo dasu
— Seigetsu

Livening the charcoal,
    now let's start
    the tea ceremony!

炭はねて始まらんとする茶の湯哉
Sumi hanete hajimaran to suru cha no yu kana
— Shiki

A solitary life;
    one flower in a vase:
    my spring.

詫住や一輪さしの花の春
Wabizumai ya ichirin sashi no hana no haru
— Koyo

How white and crisp
    this year has become,
  above the snow.

しらしらと今年になりぬ雪の上
Shirashira to kotoshi ni narinu yuki no ue
— Ito Shou

At my gate of spring,
　　the sparrows are the first
　　to greet me.

門の春雀が先へ御慶哉
Kado no haru suzume ga saki e gyokei kana

— Issa

Men going out
　　to last year's fields,
　　picking shepherd's purse.

古畑や薺摘行く男ども
Furuhata ya nazuna tsumiyuku otokodomo

— Basho

Looking carefully
　　in the hedge, shepherd's purse
　　flowers blooming.

よく見れば薺花さく垣ねかな
Yoku mireba nazuna hana saku kakine kana

— Basho

Everything and everybody,
　　even the water in the narcissus,
　　is new.

何も彼も水仙の水も新しき
Nanimokamo suisen no mizu mo atarashiki

— Shiki

Without much ado,
spring begins
this morn.

何事もなくて春たつあした哉
Nanigoto mo nakute haru tatsu ashita kana

— Inoue Shiro

An auspicious day.
But my spring?
just passable.

目出度さも中位なりおらが春
Medetasa mo chukurai nari oraga haru

— Issa

Has the New Year arrived?
In the fields,
the tracks of clogs.

正月が来たか畑に下駄の跡
Shogatsu ga kita ka hatake ni geta no ato

— Shishi Shunrai

From today,
blooming or not,
a flowery spring.

けふよりや咲ける咲かざる花の春
Kyo yori ya sakeru sakazaru hana no haru

— Nishiyama Soin

Year upon year
  I've forgotten the way home;
flowery spring.

年々や家路忘れて花の春
Nen nen ya ieji wasurete hana no haru
— Seigetsu

Hearing the temple bell,
  New Year's Day, too,
comes to a close.

元日も鐘聞く暮に及びけり
Ganjitsu mo kane kiku kure ni oyobikeri
— Hakki

In the withered tree,
  a crow;
New Year's, too, is over.

古木に鴉が、お正月もすみました
Koboku ni karasu ga, o-shogatsu mo sumimashita
— Santoka

Acknowledgments

Although it is the translator's or writer's name that appears on the cover of a book, the work is never one that has come to fruition by his or her efforts alone. In this regard, I am profoundly grateful to Kate Barnes, Jim Brems, Bill Durham, Elizabeth Frankl, Robin Gill, Gary Haskins, Takashi Ichikawa, Barry Lancet, Thomas Levidiotis, Ian McIntyre, Daniel Medvedov, Laura Nenzi, Justin Newman, John Siscoe; my late professors, Nobuo Hiraga and Richard McKinnon, Jack Whisler and many others for their support, instruction and unending encouragement over the years. And again, a special thanks to Cathy Layne at Tuttle Publishing for her dedicated and judicious editing of this anthology.

We are fortunate to have Manda's illustrations throughout this book. Her brush strokes are delicate yet decisive, and add an extra dimension to the poems along with the possibility of deeper understanding.

—William Scott Wilson

"Books to Span the East and West"

Tuttle Publishing was founded in 1832 in the small New England town of Rutland, Vermont [USA]. Our core values remain as strong today as they were then—to publish best-in-class books which bring people together one page at a time. In 1948, we established a publishing outpost in Japan—and Tuttle is now a leader in publishing English-language books about the arts, languages and cultures of Asia. The world has become a much smaller place today and Asia's economic and cultural influence has grown. Yet the need for meaningful dialogue and information about this diverse region has never been greater. Over the past seven decades, Tuttle has published thousands of books on subjects ranging from martial arts and paper crafts to language learning and literature—and our talented authors, illustrators, designers and photographers have won many prestigious awards. We welcome you to explore the wealth of information available on Asia at **www.tuttlepublishing.com**.